LIVING WITH DYSLEXIA

ABDO
Publishing Company

LIVING WITH DYSLEXIA

by Chris Eboch

Content Consultant
Vishakha Rawool
**Professor of Audiology, Department of Communication
Sciences and Disorders, West Virginia University**

LIVING WITH HEALTH CHALLENGES

CREDITS

Published by ABDO Publishing Company, PO Box 398166, Minneapolis, MN 55439. Copyright © 2014 by Abdo Consulting Group, Inc. International copyrights reserved in all countries. No part of this book may be reproduced in any form without written permission from the publisher. The Essential Library™ is a trademark and logo of ABDO Publishing Company.

Printed in the United States of America,
North Mankato, Minnesota
082013
012014

 THIS BOOK CONTAINS AT LEAST 10% RECYCLED MATERIALS.

Editor: Melissa York
Series Designer: Becky Daum

Photo credits: Apollofoto/Shutterstock Images, cover, 3; Jack Hollingsworth/Photodisc/Thinkstock, 8; Tubol Evgeniya/Shutterstock Images, 11; Lisa F. Young/Shutterstock Images, 15; Christian Jung/Shutterstock Images, 17; iStockphoto/Thinkstock, 18, 21, 29, 40, 49, 54, 57, 68, 70, 94; Blend Images/Shutterstock Images, 24; Purestock/Thinkstock, 26; Fuse/Thinkstock, 32, 59, 62, 83; Spencer Grant/Age Fotostock/SuperStock, 34; Jack Hollingsworth/Photodisc/Thinkstock, 42; Jacopin/BSIP/SuperStock, 45; JupiterImages/Thinkstock, 50, 85; Todd Warnock/Lifesize/Thinkstock, 65; Michael Jung/Shutterstock Images, 74; Monkey Business Images/Shutterstock Images, 78; F1online/Thinkstock, 87; Monkey Business/Thinkstock, 90

Library of Congress Control Number: 2013945892

Cataloging-in-Publication Data

Eboch, Chris.
 Living with dyslexia / Chris Eboch.
   p. cm. -- (Living with health challenges)
Includes bibliographical references and index.
ISBN 978-1-62403-244-8
1. Dyslexia--Juvenile literature.   I. Title.
616.85--dc23

2013945892

CONTENTS

EXPERT ADVICE

I have a master's degree in speech-language pathology, a doctorate in audiology and hearing sciences, and postdoctoral training in neurology. I am currently a professor at West Virginia University. In this role, I teach students enrolled in the Doctor of Audiology program and conduct research.

I have extensive experience working with populations ranging from infants to older adults. Some children with dyslexia have an underlying problem in processing speech sounds. As an audiologist I have seen children with sound processing issues or hearing loss. Without proper intervention, many of these children struggle with reading and writing. Children with dyslexia often have other conditions such as language impairments or attention deficit hyperactivity disorder. In the presence of such issues a teenager might struggle in forming social relationships. The problem can be made worse by cultural and linguistic differences if a child speaks a different language at home.

My advice to teenagers is:

1. Obtain a complete multidisciplinary evaluation that is conducted by individuals in the fields of audiology, speech-language pathology, reading specialists, and psychologists. In addition to the expertise in their own fields, the team members need

to be knowledgeable about the various aspects of dyslexia.

2. The results of the evaluation should be used in forming a comprehensive treatment plan that uses your existing strengths and addresses all deficits and their impact in home, educational, and other social settings.

3. Be your own advocate and make sure your individualized educational plan includes all necessary services and accommodations, as well as how often they should be provided. You should take responsibility by accepting your condition and working harder to achieve educational and social goals.

With intervention and support, many individuals with dyslexia are able to function well in academic, work, and social settings. The key factor for success is fully accepting the condition, seeking assistance as early as possible, taking advantage of treatment options, learning coping strategies to compensate for deficits that are not treatable, working harder as necessary, and developing a strong self-image with the support of family and friends.

—*Vishakha Rawool, Professor of Audiology, Department of Communication Sciences and Disorders, West Virginia University*

WHAT IS DYSLEXIA?

Jacob had always struggled in school. In-class assignments took him much longer than other students. He did better on homework because his mother helped him read the textbooks, and she checked over his answers. Tests were a nightmare, though.

*Sometimes struggling in school is a sign there
is a deeper issue, such as dyslexia or a learning
disability.*

He felt sick before every test because he knew
he would fail.

Still, he was determined to do well on his
midterm test. He spent all weekend studying
with his mother's help. Because Jacob could not
read well, his mother read the textbook chapters
out loud to him. Jacob and his mother discussed
the information until Jacob could summarize
all the important points. Then his mother asked
questions that might be on the test. After hours
of study, Jacob knew the material.

On Monday, Jacob entered the classroom
confidently. For once, he did not dread the start
of a test. He had prepared, and he was ready to
show off his knowledge.

The teacher handed out a test with 20 essay
questions. Jacob read the first question carefully
to make sure he didn't misunderstand. When he
had the question clear in his mind, he started
writing his answer.

Before he knew it, the test time was over.
Jacob had only answered two of the questions
and part of a third. Despite all his preparation,
he could not finish the test in the time given.

When Jacob got his test back, the results
were even worse than he expected. The few
answers he had provided were filled with

mistakes and spelling errors. He had failed again.

When he arrived home, Jacob's mother saw his unhappy expression and asked what was wrong. He showed her the test.

"What happened?" she asked. "You knew this material."

"I know it," Jacob said, "but I can't write what I know."

TROUBLE WITH LANGUAGE

Jacob's struggles probably sound familiar if you have dyslexia. Dyslexia is a Greek word made up of two parts. *Dys* means "difficult" or

CHECKLIST OF SYMPTOMS

If you answer yes to most of the following questions, you should get tested for dyslexia:

- Did you learn to talk late, or do you have trouble speaking clearly?
- Do you read slowly and sometimes have to read material two or three times before it makes sense?
- Are you sometimes inaccurate in reading?
- Do you find it difficult to take notes or copy material?
- Do you accidentally add or leave out letters when you are reading or writing? Do you switch letters around, putting them in the wrong order?
- Do you have difficulty planning and writing essays or letters?
- Do you have trouble remembering instructions long enough to carry out three instructions in a row?
- Do you have family members with challenges similar to those listed above?

Having dyslexia can affect how you process information, but it has nothing to do with your intelligence.

"not," and *lexis* means "words," "reading," or "language." *Dyslexia* literally means "difficulty with words."

Dyslexia is often associated with difficulty in reading, but the condition has a much broader effect. The differences in a dyslexic brain can affect how a person processes information overall. This can affect reading, writing, spelling, and other forms of communication. Individuals with dyslexia can struggle with concentrating and understanding information. If you have dyslexia, you might have trouble following directions, remembering what you've been told, and completing tasks. You probably have good days and bad days, but every day is a challenge.

If you have dyslexia, you might sometimes feel stupid. Maybe other people have even called you stupid. However, dyslexia isn't a matter of intelligence. Chances are you have normal or even above-average intelligence. Your brain wiring simply causes you to have trouble processing information. Some people might call you lazy, too. They don't understand how hard a

MYTHS ABOUT DYSLEXIA

Myth: People with dyslexia are not very intelligent.

Truth: There is no correlation between dyslexia and intelligence.

Myth: People with dyslexia reverse letters because of a visual problem.

Truth: Some individuals with dyslexia switch or reverse letters, but this is a side effect of the language processing disorder. Some individuals with dyslexia have visual processing issues even if they have normal vision or normal vision with glasses. Dyslexia has to do with brain wiring, not sight. Not all individuals who transpose letters have dyslexia.

Myth: People outgrow dyslexia.

Truth: Dyslexia is a lifelong disorder with no cure.

Myth: Dyslexia is untreatable.

Truth: Dyslexia can be treated and people with dyslexia can learn to compensate for their challenges. Accommodations help individuals participate fully in school and work.

person with dyslexia has to work to do certain things that are much easier for others. Even though you are intelligent and motivated, you might struggle to read and write as well as other people your age. You may also have trouble with math and social interactions.

DYSLEXIA VERSUS SLD

Dyslexia is what is called a specific learning difficulty (SLD). People may assume dyslexia refers primarily to reading difficulties, while SLD can cover a broader spectrum of problems. However, dyslexia is still a common term for the learning challenges associated with language and information processing.

Dyslexia is a biological difference in the way the brain works. According to some estimates, 10 to 15 percent of the US population has dyslexia. The percentage of people who have a language-based learning disability may be as high as 20 percent.[1] That's one in five people! There are many others facing the same challenges you are.

Researchers do not yet know the exact causes of dyslexia. We do know it is related to a difference in the way the brain develops and functions. It is a genetic condition that tends to run in families. Because it is a biological condition rather than a disease, there is no cure. Proper testing and treatment can ensure you receive the education that best suits your brain and learning style.

SMART BUT STRUGGLING

Dyslexia is called a learning disability because the condition can make it difficult to succeed in the standard academic environment. Yet dyslexia is not an inability to learn. Instead it is a difference in the way a person learns. You can learn just as well as anyone else, but you need different methods of instruction.

Dyslexia is not a disease. You cannot "catch" dyslexia, and it cannot be cured. If you have dyslexia, you will have it for the rest of your life. However, there are treatments that can help you overcome your weaknesses and enhance your strengths. With the right teaching methods, you can learn successfully. Unfortunately, the majority of individuals with dyslexia are never diagnosed or properly treated.

Getting a proper diagnosis of dyslexia can be complicated by other factors. If

GENDER AND DYSLEXIA

There is much debate whether dyslexia is more prevalent in boys than girls. Boys are certainly diagnosed at a higher rate, though some of this is because boys are more likely to have behavior problems too. Although some research has found boys and girls have dyslexia at the same rate, much of the newest research suggests more boys than girls are affected.

Without an accurate diagnosis or support, people with dyslexia often have trouble with schoolwork and tests.

you have attention deficit/hyperactivity disorder (ADHD), there is a 60 percent chance you also have dyslexia.[2] But parents and teachers might focus on the behavioral aspects of ADHD and fail to recognize the signs of dyslexia. Without the proper help, many people with dyslexia and ADHD are functionally illiterate, barely able to read. This limits their ability to find jobs and succeed in society. Young people with untreated dyslexia are more than twice as likely as others to drop out of high school. They are also twice as likely to become unemployed or underemployed or put in jail. By some estimates, 85 percent of illiterate adults have dyslexia.[3] Because they never received help with their dyslexia, they struggled more throughout life.

Sometimes it may hurt to be told you have a learning disability. Officially calling dyslexia a learning disability can be an advantage, however. If you have dyslexia that interferes with your education, you should qualify for special accommodations and support. This can make school easier and more enjoyable, so you can live up to your full potential. Dyslexia won't stop you from being an intelligent, creative, and successful person.

ASK YOURSELF THIS

- *What are some of the challenges people with dyslexia face? Which of these are familiar to you?*

People with dyslexia often excel at creative activities.

- *Why is dyslexia called a learning disability? How do you feel about the term* learning disability? *Does it help to have a label for any challenges you face?*

- *Do you have ADHD? If so, how does that affect your ability to learn?*

2

EXTRA CHALLENGES

Samantha was diagnosed with dyslexia in fourth grade. The diagnosis helped explain many of the problems she had in school, but it didn't immediately make things easier. Her whole family needed time to understand the situation and suggest solutions.

People with dyslexia often have to work harder to succeed in school.

And of course, Samantha still had to do her own schoolwork.

Sometimes it felt like she would never understand. She wanted to do well in her classes, but each year, the workload seemed worse. She didn't want to disappoint her parents, but could she meet their high standards?

Algebra was especially hard for her, and when Samantha got her grades, she cringed at seeing a D. She went to her teacher for advice.

Her teacher said, "You got a passing grade, and you can move on to the next level. Work hard, and I'm sure you can succeed."

Samantha thought about that as she headed home. She appreciated the teacher's encouragement, but she had doubts. Would she be able to do the extra work needed to keep up in a new math class and still complete her other homework? She also had extracurricular activities she didn't want to give up.

Samantha showed her parents her report card and quickly said, "I really did my best."

Her mother hugged her. "I saw how hard you worked. But I'm worried about next year. Maybe you should take summer classes."

Samantha groaned. "I wanted to play soccer and try that theater camp."

They set up a meeting with her tutor to discuss the matter. In the end, everyone agreed Samantha would be better off retaking the algebra class in the fall. Mastering algebra would be important to all her future math classes. Taking the class again would provide a strong foundation. Samantha wasn't looking forward to taking algebra again, but maybe it would be easier the second time around.

A RANGE OF CHALLENGES

School can be challenging for everyone, but if you have dyslexia, you must work especially hard. Sometimes the list of challenges students with dyslexia face might seem overwhelming. Learning disabilities stem from a problem in processing information. You may have been able to read and write at your grade level when you were younger but now experience problems with more complex language skills, such as

NUMBER CONFUSION

A learning disability that involves math may be referred to as dyscalculia. This condition can be due to visual-spatial difficulties. That means a person has trouble processing what their eyes see. Or dyscalculia may be a variation of language processing difficulties. In this case, a person has trouble processing and making sense of what they hear. The effects of the condition vary depending on the underlying source of the problem. Visual-spatial trouble makes it hard to visualize patterns or isolate the parts of a math problem. Language problems may cause someone to struggle with the vocabulary of math.

Dyslexia might make it difficult for you to remember lists or phone numbers.

advanced grammar. You may find it difficult to remember a list of instructions. You might struggle to organize your thoughts and express yourself clearly. You may do well in math if you have a calculator and a piece of paper but find yourself unable to remember a phone number.

Dyslexia can affect you outside the classroom as well, especially if you have other related issues. If you can't process spoken language well, you may misunderstand other people. Trouble communicating can interfere with developing social skills. In addition, if you have to spend extra time on your schoolwork, you have less time to be social. You might find it harder to connect with other students.

Some people with dyslexia can't interpret nonverbal communication very well either. Most people, over time, develop an understanding of nonverbal cues. These can include making eye contact to express interest, understanding body language, and recognizing others' personal space. If you have a learning disability, understanding these cues may not come naturally to you.

Not all people with dyslexia are alike, however. The condition can vary from mild to severe. Regardless of severity, you may excel in some areas where most people

CAN YOU READ MY WRITING?

Dysgraphia, or impaired handwriting, may appear alongside dyslexia, with other learning disabilities, or by itself. *Graph* **refers to the hand function in writing and to the letters formed by a hand. This is not a problem with how the hand functions, however. Rather, the brain has problems remembering written words, planning finger movements in order, or both. Students with dysgraphia can be treated, but the condition is often not properly diagnosed.**

with dyslexia struggle. All those with dyslexia have strengths and weaknesses.

THE EMOTIONS OF DYSLEXIA

Perhaps the worst part of dyslexia is the frustration and anxiety it can lead to. You might feel as though you are disappointing your parents and teachers. You might feel misunderstood, because you try hard but people think you are lazy or careless. You might frustrate yourself and others when you do well one day but can't repeat the task another day. If you have trouble remembering events in order, people might accuse you of lying even when you are trying to tell the truth. You might feel that no matter how hard you try, you simply cannot

FEELING SAD AND BAD

Not all people with dyslexia suffer from depression. However, people with learning disabilities are at a higher risk. People who are depressed may have negative thoughts about themselves. They also tend to view the world negatively, finding few sources of fun. Finally, young people with depression may feel hopeless about the future. They might have little to look forward to because they expect to fail. Children and teenagers with dyslexia may try to cover up painful feelings by misbehaving. This can make it harder for others to recognize their depression.

You can seek help for depression. Talk to your parents, counselor, doctor, or another trusted adult if you feel depressed. It can help to celebrate successes or to reach out to others through volunteer work.

The stresses of having dyslexia can leave some people feeling frustrated or unhappy.

succeed. All this can lead to feelings of sadness or anger.

Sometimes students with dyslexia react to the challenges of school by trying to do less. You might think that if you don't do any writing, you can avoid spelling mistakes. Or you might stay away from new situations because you expect failure. It might even be tempting to drop out of school to avoid academic challenges. It's important to understand that with help and hard work, you can succeed. By working hard now, you set yourself up for a better life. The key is getting the support you need.

ASK YOURSELF THIS

- *How can dyslexia affect your ability to interact with other people? Have you felt confused or left out in social interactions?*

- *How can dyslexia affect your emotions? Have you experienced negative feelings like frustration, sadness, or anger?*

- *How do you react to school stress? Do you ask for help, keep working on your own, or avoid tough situations?*

- *What do you believe your strengths are? What do you do to take advantage of your strengths?*

- *What do you believe your weaknesses are? What do you do to work around your weaknesses?*

3

THE BRIGHT SIDE OF DYSLEXIA

Lamont's favorite class has always been art. At the start of the school year, his counselor helped him find an art mentor. Lamont was nervous about their first meeting. Why would a professional artist want to hang out with a kid who wasn't even a good student?

It is important for people with dyslexia to find their strengths and pursue them.

But the artist, a painter and sculptor named Cindy, greeted Lamont with a friendly smile. "Is that your sketchbook?" she asked.

Lamont nodded and offered the sketchbook. He held his breath while Cindy flipped through the pages. Finally Cindy said, "You have some real talent. What do you want to do with your art in the future?"

"I'd like to go into either graphic design or computer animation, if I can."

"Good choices," Cindy said. "Let me show you what I'm working on, and then we can come up with a project for you. We'll meet once a week and work together."

After that first meeting, Lamont wasn't nervous about going to Cindy's studio. Lamont learned how to be a better artist, and he also saw what is involved in a professional art career. He began dreaming of going to art school. Knowing he had that option helped him stay focused on doing well in his classes.

Lamont also learned to use visual cues in other areas. He found that using color codes on his calendar helped him stay organized. Small drawings worked better than words to remind him of tasks to do. He was a natural artist. Realizing this, Lamont started to feel better about himself. He realized if he could succeed in art, he could succeed in other areas of his life. He did not have to be a failure, even if he could not read or write well.

A WELL-ROUNDED LIFE

When you focus on all the negative ways dyslexia can affect your life, you might feel as though you have been cursed. However, not all aspects of dyslexia are bad. Dyslexia may make school harder, but you can still be a bright, talented, and creative person. You have some natural strengths, and you may develop additional strengths as you find ways to handle your dyslexia. In fact, some people even believe dyslexia should be considered an asset, not a disability.

People with dyslexia are a diverse group. Their individual strengths

DYSLEXIA ON STAGE

Actor Orlando Bloom was diagnosed with dyslexia at age seven. Although he had to work especially hard in school, he had a natural acting talent and good leadership skills. He joined Britain's National Youth Theatre at age 16 and appeared on television before age 20. He then earned fame for his roles in the Lord of the Rings and Pirates of the Caribbean movie series. Giving advice to others with dyslexia, Bloom said, "Take this obstacle and make it the reason to have a big life."[1] Other famous actors with dyslexia include Tom Cruise, Will Smith, Whoopi Goldberg, Keanu Reeves, Keira Knightley, and Vince Vaughn.

Some people with dyslexia prefer working with their hands.

vary as much as their specific challenges. While some have visual processing problems, others may be more visually oriented, and therefore good with their hands. Many people with dyslexia have a good visual eye, which may express itself as artistic talent. They are often creative and may have an excellent imagination. They may also be good with arts and crafts.

Some people with dyslexia may also excel at practical skills such as repairing computers or cars. Students with dyslexia often do well in science, math, computer programming, and technology. No single strength is present in all people with dyslexia, but every individual has some strengths.

LEADING THE WORLD

Some individuals with dyslexia are creative and empathetic people who see the big picture. This can be an advantage for people in many fields, including business. Researcher Julie Logan studied individuals with dyslexia who were also entrepreneurs. She said, "The ability to attack problems and solve them is essential when one is creating a new venture, so the [student with dyslexia] who has had to overcome problems to survive at school has much experience in this area."[2]

The skills you learn for dealing with your dyslexia can apply in the working world. Stu Shader did poorly in school

SOCIAL SKILLS

Although some people with dyslexia struggle with social skills, others can be very charming. For some, social ability may come naturally, while others may learn skills as they grow up. Someone who struggles to read aloud from notes may develop strong speaking skills to compensate. Many adults with dyslexia consider their social skills to be a key to their success.

Rob Langston is a motivational speaker who gives programs on dyslexia. In his book *For the Children: Redefining Success in School and Success in Life*, he says, "My first advice to anyone labeled in these ways is to STOP. Rethink. Change your self-description from 'learning-disabled' to 'learning-abled.' Today I still read at the seventh grade level, but I am an extremely 'able' speaker, so that I can make my living that way!"[3]

and barely graduated from high school. Yet he has worked for large technology companies, including Microsoft and Apple. He learned to accommodate his dyslexia through techniques such as sitting in the front row during meetings. He also brought his special strengths to the job. He can see the big picture, communicates well, and can simplify information for his clients.

MANY SMARTS

IQ tests, and our school system, are generally designed to test ability with words and with numbers. However, some people think there are other kinds of intelligence. Is musical ability a different kind of intelligence? How about athletic ability or an awareness of shapes and how things fit together? Interpersonal intelligence is

BUSINESS SUCCESS

Ben Foss is a successful businessman with an MBA and a law degree from Stanford University. He has worked for the Children's Defense Fund and the White House National Economic Council. In an interview, Foss said,

Because of my dyslexia I functioned well in these professional environs. I learned to pay attention to what matters in an academic or professional setting. I knew that I could not read an entire book, so I would prioritize, reading only the most important chapter. In the White House, no one has enough time, so being able to prioritize and delegate is critical. I also learned to engage people and understand their roles.[4]

Foss now leads a team that makes tools to help people who have trouble reading printed text.

Practice your strengths, whether it's science, acting, sports, public speaking, or anything in between.

the ability to understand others. Intrapersonal intelligence is the ability to understand oneself. Even spiritual and moral intelligence have been suggested as possible types of intelligence. Any person, dyslexic or not, may have strengths in one area and weaknesses in another.

Unfortunately, programs for students with dyslexia often focus on trying to overcome weaknesses. If you spend all your time focusing on areas where you struggle, your self-esteem can suffer. It is important you also find ways to identify and nurture your strengths. This could mean participating in extracurricular activities or classes such as art, music, and drama. If your school does not offer these classes or clubs, seek them out in the community. You could even try to start your own band, comedy group, or photography club.

Psychiatrist Dr. Ned Hallowell says,

> *I have learned first and foremost to look for interests, talents, strengths, shades of strengths, or the mere suggestion of a talent. Knowing that a person builds a happy and successful life not on remediated weaknesses but on developed strengths, I have learned to place those strengths at the top of what matters.*[5]

Make accommodations for your weak areas and also celebrate your assets. That's the way to be most successful in school and in life.

ASK YOURSELF THIS

- *What kinds of intelligence are there? Do you feel more intelligent in some areas than others?*

- *How do your strengths relate to your weaknesses or challenges?*

- *Have you tried many activities, such as different sports, art, music, and theater? Are there other areas you would like to explore?*

- *How might your strengths help you in the future?*

4

TESTING AND DIAGNOSIS

Rosa enjoyed school and did well for the first few years. She had some trouble reading, but her parents assumed this was due to the normal variation in how children learn. But as the material became more complicated, Rosa found herself falling behind. She hid in the back of the classroom to avoid the teacher's attention. She knew she was disappointing her parents, and she couldn't make them understand she was trying her hardest. Embarrassed by her grades, she withdrew from her friends.

Finally a teacher asked for a meeting with Rosa's parents. Rosa dreaded the meeting, but she never expected what the teacher said. "When I talk to Rosa, I can tell she is a bright child. But I wonder if she has a learning disability that is making schoolwork difficult for her. Would you consider getting her tested?" Her parents asked some questions and then agreed.

Rosa went into the test shaking with anxiety. The tester chatted with her for a while, helping put Rosa at ease. She said, "Try to relax and not worry about your scores." The tester then gave her a variety of activities, including answering oral questions and working with puzzles. The whole test took approximately three hours. Rosa was tired by the end, but mostly it had been fun.

After the test, Rosa and her family discussed the results with a counselor who was an expert on dyslexia. The counselor helped Rosa's teachers understand the situation. Together they came up with a plan to make school better for Rosa.

IDENTIFY THE PROBLEM

If you suspect you have dyslexia, there are good reasons to get tested. For one, an evaluation is required before your school can provide any special education services. In addition, every person with a learning disability is slightly different, so an evaluation can identify your individual needs. Motivational speaker Rob Langston, who speaks on dyslexia, says, "Testing and documentation are essential and powerful tools. They help learning disabled students get what they need from the educational system. Testing leaves a paper trail. . . . The documentation becomes your foundation for getting services and accommodations."[1]

US law provides free testing in special education services for public school children.

WHO CAN DIAGNOSE DYSLEXIA?

Teachers or family members may be the first people to suspect a child has a learning disability. However, the diagnosis is complicated and should be made by professionals. Ideally a team of people with different specialties will conduct a series of tests. Testers should have experience in hearing, reading, language, education, and psychology. They must understand the proper way to administer the test and interpret data. Finally, only experts can offer the best plan for helping the student based on the test results.

The Individuals with Disabilities Education Act (IDEA) identifies a number of disabilities. If a child needs special education and related services because of a disability, IDEA ensures the child receives help. IDEA lays out the rights parents have when it comes to educational evaluation.

Parents who want their child tested can contact the school principal, a teacher, or the director of special education for the school district. If the school agrees an evaluation is necessary, it will provide the testing at no cost. In some cases, families find it is better to find the expert themselves rather than relying on their school. Schools may resist expensive testing or may have a long waiting list. If you have trouble getting help through the school, you can ask your family doctor for a referral to a testing expert.

MORE LEGAL HELP

Some young people have a disability that does not require extra educational assistance, at least according to their tests. These children are not eligible for help under IDEA. However, Section 504 of the Rehabilitation Act and the Americans with Disabilities Act (ADA) provide additional protections.

Federal and state laws are in place to protect children with learning disabilities. If parents or guardians feel their child is not getting the proper help, they can consult the law or speak to a lawyer.

WHAT TO EXPECT

Do not be afraid of these tests. They will
help you get the support you need to learn
and succeed. You can be tested at any age.
Ideally, dyslexia is caught early so intervention
can begin while a child is young. However,
some people are not diagnosed until they are
teenagers or even adults. Getting a diagnosis
can still help you address the problem.

No single test can clearly identify dyslexia.
For a proper diagnosis, you should get a
thorough differential diagnosis. This series of
tests considers the entire range of dyslexia and
attention deficit disorders. The tests will study
how you express and understand spoken and
written language. They will check how well you
see and hear. They will look at your intelligence
and how well you follow information. They will
also consider your family history, your education
so far, and other factors that might affect how
you learn.

The evaluator or team of experts will look
for other problems as well. It is important to rule
out other disorders that share symptoms with
dyslexia. These include physical or sensory
impairments such as vision or hearing problems.
ADHD and conditions such as anxiety and
depression can also cause symptoms similar to
dyslexia.

It is possible to have both dyslexia and other disorders. In that case, you will need to receive treatment for every condition. For example, if you have a hearing problem, that should be addressed first. If you have ADHD, you might benefit from prescription medication. Your dyslexia supports might be less helpful if other underlying conditions are not treated.

WHAT'S NEXT

After testing, your family should receive a written report with the test scores and an explanation of the results. The report will have specific suggestions based on your own needs. You should then have a team meeting with the testers, your teachers, and your family. Together this team can work out a plan of action.

NO QUICK CURES

When you have dyslexia or a similar condition, it is tempting to want a quick cure. Many people and programs offer impressive promises. However, just because someone claims a therapy works doesn't mean it is true. Beware of any promise that sounds too good to be true or that is based on secret formulas. Another warning sign is a promise of success for all users, since no treatment works for everyone. Some treatments are based on small studies that may be promising but need further investigation. The best treatments are those that have been tested extensively with many subjects over time. Other treatments may, at best, be a waste of time and money. At worst, they could be dangerous. Consult with experts before trying experimental therapies.

Getting tested will help your school make a plan to adapt to your learning needs.

Do not expect immediate changes. Schools may be slow to put new accommodations into place. Some teachers may have difficulty changing their teaching style. Your family members may be excited about a diagnosis that explains your behavior, but they may also be anxious. You may be nervous about all these changes as well. Everyone will need time to adjust to a diagnosis of dyslexia.

If you are diagnosed with a learning disability, that first test is not the end. You must be evaluated at least every three years. Each evaluation determines if you still need special services. Proper testing is essential so you get the help you need throughout life.

ASK YOURSELF THIS

- *Have you been tested for dyslexia? If so, how did it change your life?*

- *If you have not been tested, do you think you should be? Why or why not?*

- *Would you recommend a dyslexia test to other people? If so, under what conditions? If not, why not?*

- *Do you have any health challenges or conditions besides dyslexia that interfere with your schoolwork? Are you getting the help you need with those problems?*

WHAT'S HAPPENING IN MY BRAIN?

During the first week of school, Marcus misspelled his middle name on a paper. Instead of *Brian*, he wrote *Brain*. When the teacher handed back the paper, he chuckled and said, "What kind of brain can't even spell his own name?" Marcus pretended he didn't care about the teasing, but inside he felt humiliated. It didn't help when some of the other kids started calling him "Brain" and laughing.

Marcus wanted to tell them making mistakes like that did not mean he was stupid. He got decent grades, most of the time. He excelled at a lot of other things, too. He was a star soccer player and inspired others as team captain. He was smart and capable, even though he struggled sometimes in school.

However, he often had trouble explaining his dyslexia to other people. He knew his brain worked differently, but it was normal to him. He knew other students had an easier time reading and writing, but he could not really imagine their experiences. How could he make people understand and respect him?

Marcus told his mother what happened with the teacher. She was angry at first, but finally she sighed and said, "Sometimes adults are careless, just like kids. Let's set up a meeting and make sure your teacher understands the situation." She set up a meeting with the teacher and Marcus's tutor to discuss Marcus's dyslexia. Once he understood the situation, the teacher related to Marcus in a new way. He demanded hard work, but he was encouraging. In fact, he became one of Marcus's favorite teachers.

WHAT WE KNOW NOW

Doctors first described dyslexia more than 100 years ago. However, dyslexia was not widely understood or even recognized until the 1990s. Many people assumed children who showed the symptoms of dyslexia were stupid or lazy. Sometimes dyslexia was blamed on emotional or family problems. However, research has shown most preschoolers with dyslexia are happy and well adjusted. Any emotional problems they develop are due to struggling in school, not directly because of dyslexia.

Research on the brain helps us better understand dyslexia and how to treat it. There are many differences between human brains, and they are not necessarily related to learning disabilities. However, brain studies have shown some typical differences in dyslexic brains.

The brain is mainly made up of gray matter and white matter. Gray matter is primarily nerve cells that process information. White matter is found deeper in the brain. It is made of connective fibers with a coating that helps the nerves communicate. White matter allows information to transfer between areas of the brain.

One study found people with dyslexia have less gray matter in specific areas of the brain. Many also have differences in the white matter compared to average readers. Individuals with

BRAIN

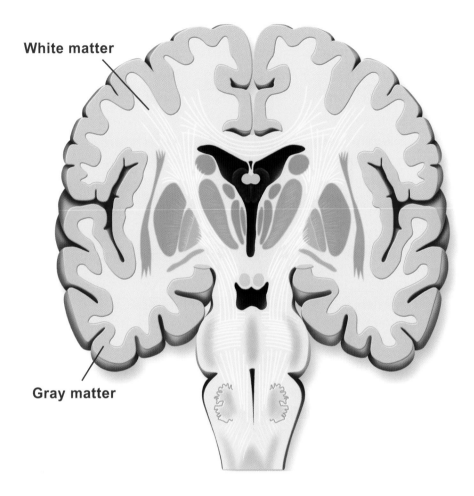

White matter

Gray matter

dyslexia may also have different brain symmetry. Most right-handed, non-dyslexic people have larger left hemispheres. Right-handed people with dyslexia tend to have hemispheres of equal size, or a larger right side. Scientists do not yet know why these differences occur, but they help explain why those with dyslexia have different abilities.

LOOKING INSIDE YOUR MIND

In order to understand brain function, researchers need to be able to watch brain activity. Functional magnetic resonance imaging (fMRI) is one technique used. The *functional* in fMRI means the patient functions, or performs tasks, during the test. The tasks might include answering questions about images or sounds or making simple motions such as touching your thumb to your fingers. A strong magnet pinpoints blood flow, showing how the brain is reacting. This allows researchers to see the brain in action, rather than at rest.

Your brain is less active when you are doing tasks you don't do well. Children with dyslexia do not have as much activation in areas important for reading as other children. However, people with dyslexia often show more activity in a

THE BRAIN ON CAMERA

While fMRI machines are helpful for studying the brain, they are not used for diagnosing dyslexia. One problem is that fMRI machines are expensive. They also require expensive computers, software, and staff to run the studies and interpret the results. In addition, participants must keep their heads completely still during the study. This is difficult for young children.

Finally, the data revealed by an fMRI is less useful in diagnosing an individual person. Studies so far have focused on differences across groups of people.

different area of the brain. Because some areas of their brains do not work as well, they may compensate by using other areas. These other systems may not be as efficient, though. That might explain why even those who can read accurately are still slow. Their brains must work harder, so they don't work as quickly.

One of the surprises of brain research is how common dyslexia is. Some estimates have been as low as 5 percent of the population.[1] However, one study of a random sample of Connecticut schoolchildren found approximately 20 percent of the group had dyslexia.[2]

READING AND YOUR BRAIN

The brain can be divided into a right and a left hemisphere. Most of the areas involved in speech, reading, and language processing are in the left hemisphere. Each hemisphere has four lobes. All four lobes in the left hemisphere are involved in language processing as well as other tasks.

The frontal lobe controls speech, reasoning, and planning. Some areas are important for silent reading.

The parietal lobe links spoken and written language to memory. This is necessary so we can understand what we hear and read.

The occipital lobe is involved in sight and visual perception. This is important in the identification of letters.

The temporal lobe is involved in processing what you hear, including spoken language.

Two other systems process language within and between lobes. The left parietotemporal system helps in analyzing and decoding words. The left occipitotemporal area is critical for fluent reading.

LEARNING WHAT WORKS

Brain studies are helpful in identifying useful treatments for dyslexia. Researchers can look at brain activity before and after a treatment to see the effects. Some early studies have shown increased brain activity in students with dyslexia who are receiving special tutoring.

Brain studies are limited so far. Test subjects must not move their heads during the study, so they can only think about their answers. fMRI cannot be used to study tasks such as reading aloud. Technological advances might allow a greater range of tests in the future.

Scientists all over the world are studying dyslexia. As the condition is better understood, new treatments may arise. It's important to keep track of current research if you want the best chance to overcome dyslexia. You can share what you learn with others, so they can understand and help you.

ASK YOURSELF THIS

- *What mistaken ideas have people had about dyslexia? Do you run into misconceptions like these today?*

- *How can fMRI teach us about brain function? Have you had a brain test? What did you learn about your brain?*

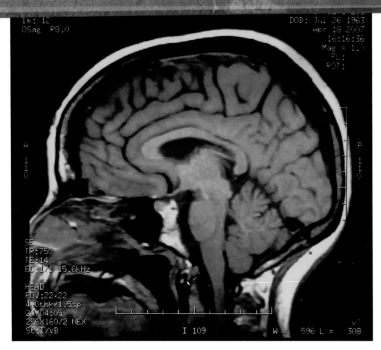

Researchers can learn a lot about the human brain using MRI scans.

- *How are the brains of people with dyslexia and non-dyslexic people different? If your brain is "different," how do you feel about that?*

- *Why is it important to study dyslexia and the treatments being used? Would you want to join one of these studies? Why or why not?*

6

DYSLEXIA AT SCHOOL

E mma copied down the assignment her teacher wrote on the board. This included a password so students could access the school computer system from home. But when Emma tried to log in at home, she got an error message.

For many students, having dyslexia means they have to work harder than their classmates.

The following day at school, Emma told her teacher the password had not worked. Her teacher looked at Emma's notes and said, "That is not the correct password. You need to be more careful."

Emma had dyslexia, so she needed to take more time with her work. She and her teachers were still figuring out the proper balance between pushing Emma and giving her help. Sometimes this was a matter of trial and error. Emma was allowed to take more time for her tests. In some classes, she took her tests orally. One teacher allowed her to finish in-class assignments at home. But her teachers wanted her to succeed in life, so they demanded quality work.

Emma had to find ways to work with all of her teachers. When teachers were inflexible, Emma's mother met with them to make sure they understood Emma's needs. In a few cases, she requested that Emma be moved to a different class. However, most teachers were happy to work with Emma. Once they understood her situation, they tried to find ways to both challenge and support her.

Emma sometimes envied her friends who did not seem to work so hard. But Emma realized everyone has strengths and

A SPECIAL SCHOOL

Most school programs for people with dyslexia focus on trying to help the person fit into the traditional school system. However, a different educational system may be better suited to the dyslexic learning style. The Assets School is a private school for children with dyslexia, gifted children, and gifted children with dyslexia in Honolulu, Hawaii.

All students receive regular individual and group counseling. Classes involve more hands-on activities and integrate art, music, reading, writing, and science. Students choose among enrichment courses that explore different areas of interest, including arts, science, math, computers, athletics, and other offerings. In addition, a mentoring program allows students to work with members of the community.

weaknesses. She also knew she could attend college to pursue her dream. She wanted to become a special education teacher so she could help other struggling students.

FINDING WHAT WORKS FOR YOU

If you have dyslexia, you'll face special challenges at school. The first step is getting a clear diagnosis. Then make sure your teachers and the principal are ready to work with you.

The most common treatment is to modify the educational environment to meet the needs of a person with dyslexia. The basis of this education involves two principles. First is instruction in phonemic awareness. Second is learning phonics. This training must be intense and long lasting to be effective.

Chances are, some of your teachers understand your dyslexia better than others. You may need to spend time educating those who are less familiar with the condition. There are many resources available to help teachers understand the needs of students with dyslexia. Do not hesitate to point teachers toward this information or ask for what you need.

You may prefer teachers who explain things in a clear, simple manner. Most people with dyslexia do better with structured daily routines. It will help teachers to do daily reviews of previous material. You may also learn best with a mix of teaching techniques, such as visual, oral, and hands-on activities.

THE INDIVIDUALIZED EDUCATION PROGRAM

The Individuals with Disabilities Education Act (IDEA) guides special education. A child who receives special education services under IDEA must have an Individualized Education Program (IEP). A team including the school staff and the student's parents or guardians develops a student's IEP. Older students also can participate in the planning. This written document lists the special education services the child will receive from the school. It describes the student's level of academic achievement and how the student's disability affects his or her progress. It also sets reasonable learning goals for the student.

In high school, IEP meetings should address transition services. These services are designed to help you plan for your life after high school.

Don't be afraid to talk to teachers about what they can do to work with your condition.

You might be allowed to use a tape recorder to record lessons and directions. You can then replay the tape later to make sure you understand. Or perhaps your teacher can give you a written copy rather than asking you to write down material from the board or take notes in class. They may give you a glossary of terms important to what you are studying. A reading guide can direct you to helpful material. Assignment books, calendars, and graphic organizers will help you stay organized.

Some schools provide accessible instructional materials (AIM) to qualified students. They can be provided in audio or digital formats. Audio formats can be either a recorded human voice or synthesized electronic speech. Digital files use reading software so the user can hear a computer voice read the text.

In addition, many digital devices can be used at home. Computers, e-readers, and smartphones allow for reading digital formats

DISPUTE RESOLUTIONS

You, your parents or guardians, and teachers and school employees should work together to make sure you receive appropriate services. However, sometimes your family may feel you are not getting what you deserve. Your first option should be to try politely to work out the situation. This could involve asking for a review of your IEP to discuss concerns. Sometimes it helps to have a facilitator at the meeting. A facilitator's task is to keep the team focused on goals and not take sides.

If a team meeting does not solve the problem, you have other options. In mediation, family members and school employees meet to discuss the issues. A mediator helps the parties communicate openly and respectfully.

If all else fails, you can file a state complaint. This should describe what requirements of the IDEA law the school has violated. If the school system failed in its duties, it must take steps to correct the problem.

aloud. Students with dyslexia also benefit from other software tools. Voice recognition allows you to dictate essays. Other software has helpful tools such as note-taking functions, dictionaries, and search features.

CUTTING OUT DISTRACTIONS

Some students with dyslexia may benefit from an FM system. The teacher wears a microphone and a transmitter. The student wears a receiving unit and earphones. The FM system projects the teacher's voice directly to the child's ears, cutting out other classroom noises. This helps the child hear clearly and focus on the information.

In one study, after one year of using the FM system, children with dyslexia showed improvement in several areas. They had better reading skills and understanding of language. Their brains also responded more consistently to sounds. A matched group of children with dyslexia without the FM device did not show such improvements.

SPECIAL TRAINING

Your test for dyslexia may show you need additional instruction. In that case, you may be sent to a special class or receive individual tutoring. Your tutor should have special training in working with students with dyslexia. Don't hesitate to ask about the tutor's training and experience, or encourage your family to do so. You also need to feel comfortable working with this instructor. It takes time to

It's important to find a tutor with whom you can build a strong relationship.

get used to a new situation, so don't judge too quickly. However, if you continue to feel uncomfortable with the teacher, you may want to request a change. Developing a bond with your instructor will make the sessions more enjoyable and effective.

Your tutoring is likely to last a long time. Students with dyslexia advance the most when they have regular, ongoing special instruction. This may be two to five sessions per week, for up to two hours per session, for several years.

This steady practice will help you master skills and apply them on your own.

Depending on your schedule, you may meet before school, during the school day, or after school. To get the most out of your specialized instruction, meet at a time when you are alert. Be sure to attend these sessions whenever possible. The more sessions you miss, the harder it will be for you to make steady progress.

YOU ARE IN CHARGE!

If you don't qualify for accommodations under current laws and guidelines, you may still be able to get help. Discuss your needs with your teachers. You may have to prove you can succeed if given accommodations. For example, if you are failing tests, you might ask to be tested orally after class. If you can then prove to the teacher you know the material, he or she might be willing to give all your tests orally.

Teachers may be more willing to work with you if you explain what you will do in return. Let them know you will come to class prepared, participate fully, and give 100 percent. Then follow through on those promises. If you make your teachers' jobs easier, they will find it easier to help you.

You should take control of your own education. Clear and frequent communication is

You may be able to ask for accommodations in the classroom to help you learn and demonstrate what you know.

key. If you are having trouble, talk to someone. If you are afraid of failing or you are avoiding something because it is difficult, ask for help. Talking about your concerns can help relieve some of the stress. You may also find teachers, your parents, or others have ideas that could help. Teachers are busy with dozens or hundreds of students. If they forget what they

THE COST OF TRAINING

Working with an educational specialist outside of school may cost money. Fees vary depending on where you live and the professional's qualifications. The specialist may charge extra to come to your home. Instructional materials could cost more. Some professionals also charge for school meetings or phone calls.

Your family is responsible for asking about these fees and arranging for payment. The cost of specialized instruction may be covered by your family's health insurance. Some services are tax deductible. You can also ask your school for help finding grants and scholarships.

have agreed to in the past, politely remind them.

Many resources are available for people with dyslexia and their families. These can help you understand your condition and navigate the school system. They can also connect you with support groups for other teenagers and adults with dyslexia. Knowing you are not alone and there are people who understand what you are going through can be a comfort.

ASK YOURSELF THIS

- *What kind of instruction should a student with dyslexia get? How can this happen inside and outside of the classroom? What are your experiences with special classes or tutoring?*

- *Why are some teachers better than others for a student with dyslexia? What qualities would you want in your ideal teacher?*

- *What kind of accommodations can help students with dyslexia? Have you tried any of these? Did they make a difference for you?*

- *What can you do if you are not getting the help you need in school? If you don't qualify for accommodations under the law, what are your options?*

- *Where can you get more help and advice? Why is this important? Have you ever tried to connect with a support group?*

7

HELP AT HOME

Anthony struggled throughout elementary school. When he was diagnosed with dyslexia and ADHD, his father was relieved to have an explanation for his behavior. Anthony soon realized there was an advantage, too—he could get away with doing less work.

Don't let dyslexia prevent you from working to your full potential.

If he scored poorly on an assignment, his father would say, "That's all right. You have dyslexia." Anthony no longer faced so much pressure to get good grades.

As he entered high school, Anthony was behind most of his friends academically. While they took advanced classes and were thinking about college, he was stuck in remedial classes where he was bored. Anthony realized he had been using his dyslexia as an excuse. He knew he might have to work harder than his friends to do as well, but he could do the work if he tried.

Anthony began studying harder and exploring different learning techniques. He found tools that allowed him to listen to text out loud and use dictation to write papers. As he did better in his classes, his teachers expected more of him. Anthony rose to meet these higher expectations.

When he brought home a report card that had mostly Bs, his father simply stared. Then he grinned and slapped Anthony on the back. "Good work," he said. "Let's go out to celebrate." Over pizza, they started talking about the future. Anthony's father said, "I always wanted to be an architect, but my grades were bad. I don't mind what I'm doing, but you could do better. You could be the first in the family to go to college!"

"I'm not sure what I want to be yet," Anthony said. "But I'll figure it out." At least now he knew he had options.

WORKING TOGETHER

When you are diagnosed with dyslexia, it affects your whole family. Your parents or guardians may not always know the best thing to do. They may be worried about your future. You can help each other by communicating clearly. You should try to talk about your school experiences so your parents can understand what you are going through. Together you can learn how to handle your dyslexia.

Ideally, your parents or guardians will be your allies and advocates in your education. They can help you make informed decisions and support you through your struggles. They can make sure you do your homework, offer assistance when necessary, and help you practice for tests. They can remind you to take any medication for other conditions such as ADHD and check that you have what you need for the school day. They can set realistic goals and high expectations for you. They can check in with your teachers regularly to keep track of your progress. They can step in when you are not getting the help you need. All of these things can help you succeed in school.

Your parents can help you manage your dyslexia.

FINDING A BALANCE

If you have more than one adult involved in your life, they may not always agree on what is best for you. Sometimes you may feel torn between different opinions. Remember adults are human too. Even when they are trying to do their best, they can make mistakes. They may be frustrated or impatient sometimes. Try to talk openly about your needs and concerns, and encourage your family members to share their feelings as well. Support groups can help you navigate these difficult relationships.

Adults may focus on helping you succeed academically. However, it is also important to celebrate and develop your strengths. You are more likely to feel motivated in areas where you do well. Your parents or guardians can help you find activities you enjoy. These may include sports, school clubs, and community classes. You can also explore Web sites and books on your favorite topics, or meet with others who share your interests.

There are as many different types of parents as there are types of students with dyslexia. Some parents don't make education a high priority or don't know how to support their children's education. Maybe one or both of your parents also have dyslexia. They may have struggled in school and may be intimidated meeting with your

DIET AND DYSLEXIA

Eating a healthy diet is important for many reasons. Studies on mice suggest diet might even affect ADHD and some learning disabilities. Some groups claim people with dyslexia are more susceptible to allergies, including food sensitivities. Scientific studies have not found evidence of this so far. Some families report that eliminating certain foods from the diet, or taking supplements, helps with ADHD. However, studies have not shown a definite effect on learning disabilities.

Still, dietary changes may help you feel better overall so you can do your best work. You can try dietary changes with the advice of a physician or nutrition expert. Healthful eating may make you feel better physically and mentally, but do not go to extremes. A healthful, well-balanced diet is important, but it is not a cure for learning disabilities.

teachers. They may find it hard to understand the information on your condition. They may be distracted by other problems in their own lives. If you don't have support at home, do not give up. Find a teacher or school counselor who can speak up for you.

If you have siblings, your dyslexia can also affect them. A sibling may become angry or jealous because you are receiving extra attention. Your parents may expect more from your siblings or demand they help you. That can be frustrating for someone who simply wants to be a kid. At the same time, you may resent a sibling who seems to have an easier life than you do. Once again, your best tool is communication. Express your feelings calmly,

HOMESCHOOLING

The traditional school system is not always a good fit for a student with dyslexia. Homeschooling allows for individualized instruction in all subject areas. The student can focus on areas of interest and work at a comfortable pace.

There are major challenges with homeschooling a student with dyslexia. These students do best with specific kinds of education, and the home teacher may not be properly trained. Planning lessons can require intensive research. Students with dyslexia may also do well with art, music, and sports, which can be hard to provide at home. These options may be available through field trips and homeschooling support groups that share resources.

Not all families can manage homeschooling. Another option is home tutoring in addition to regular school.

Even if they don't have dyslexia as well, your siblings can feel affected by your condition.

with respect for the people around you. Be willing to listen to others and try to understand how they feel.

Dyslexia runs in families, so if you have dyslexia, you may not be the only one. You can use your knowledge to help identify the problem in others. This could help younger siblings or cousins get an early diagnosis. It's possible your parents or grandparents had dyslexia but were never diagnosed. Learning about the condition may help them understand the challenges they have faced in school and on the job. You can offer advice from your own experience.

Your family members can be your best allies in tackling dyslexia. However, don't use dyslexia as an excuse—and don't let your family members expect less of you because of it. In the end, you are the one most responsible for your own success.

ASK YOURSELF THIS

- *How can family members help a student with dyslexia succeed in school? How has your family helped you?*

- *What are some conflicts that can arise between family members? Have you faced some of these in your family? What can you do about them?*

- *Why is it important to celebrate strengths as well as weaknesses? How can you explore more areas of interest? Can your family help?*

- *What is the best way to communicate with people? Are you a good communicator? What could you try to do differently?*

8

COPING AND SUPPORT

When Victoria's family moved, she
started at a new school. Because she
was friendly and outgoing, she made
friends quickly. She hesitated to tell them about
her dyslexia, though. She worried they would
tease her or not want to be friends.

It might be difficult to decide how much to tell your friends about your dyslexia.

One day after school, her friends were going to play a new video game. When they settled around the game console, Rachel offered Victoria the first try. She was good at video games, so she was happy to show off her abilities.

A screen came up filled with instructions. Victoria stared at the writing, but she couldn't make sense of it. She knew it would take her far too long to wade through all that material. Her friends would know something was wrong with her.

Finally Victoria turned to Rachel and said, "I have dyslexia. It means I don't read very well. Could you help me out and read these instructions?"

Victoria held her breath as she waited for Rachel's response. Finally Rachel said, "Sure, I can read the instructions to you."

Victoria relaxed and turned her attention back to the game as Rachel read. Maybe her friends didn't care if she had dyslexia. Later, she could ask if they had questions and explain in more detail. It would be nice to be able to talk about it.

A CONSTANT COMPANION

Your dyslexia influences many aspects of your life. It can affect how you do in school and how you relate to your teachers. Your challenges concern your parents or guardians, your siblings, and possibly other relatives.

You may be frustrated by people who tell you to "try harder" when you are trying as hard as you can. On the other hand, sometimes you may feel as though everyone is treating you like a child. As you grow older, it can be hard to make people understand what you are capable of doing on your own.

Dyslexia can affect your friendships and romantic relationships as well. Friends and potential dates might not understand the way you think. They may get frustrated if you forget plans or don't always follow what they mean. You might find yourself growing apart from your old friends as they take different classes. You might feel awkward in social situations and be slow to make new friends. If you have to spend more time studying or getting tutored, you will not have as much time for a social life. Sometimes you might feel left out if you can't do things others do easily.

All teenagers struggle with these issues to some extent. But if you have dyslexia, your parents may be overprotective and hesitant to let you venture out on your own. You may need to ask for more responsibility and freedom at times. It's also important to recognize when you need help and ask for it without embarrassment. You will have the best chance of getting what you want if you can explain clearly and calmly.

Try to set realistic goals for yourself, without expecting perfection. If you are not sure what is realistic, ask for help. Try to keep a positive attitude as you strive for those goals, even when it feels as though you are not making progress. All these skills take time to develop, but you will get better with practice.

If you are struggling with feelings of anxiety, anger, or depression, talk to someone. If the first person you talk to does not seem to understand

EXPLAINING YOUR NEEDS

Businessman Ben Foss initially kept his learning disability a secret, even though that meant he got less help than he needed. In business school at Stanford, he met a fellow student who had no hands. Foss explained, "I learned from him that giving people context on how to deal with you as a person with a disability is critical. He sent a [message] to everyone at the school explaining, 'Hi, I am Mark. I have no hands. When you meet me, shake my wrist. If you see me in class, I do not need your help picking up my bag. I brought it in with me in the first place . . .' and so on. It showed me that if you explain who you are and what you need, people generally are open to it."[1]

It can be frustrating if your friends, family, or teachers don't understand what your capabilities are.

or have time for you, don't give up. Find another relative, teacher, or friend. Anyone who is willing to listen and be supportive can help. Other people with dyslexia might be your best resource, since they understand what you're going through from experience. If they are successfully managing their dyslexia, they might have ideas that will help you. A professional counselor can also help you get the tools you need to communicate with other people. Support groups can offer advice and help you meet people who understand your situation.

HELP OTHERS, HELP YOURSELF

Not so long ago, dyslexia was poorly understood. Today we know much more about the condition, and people with dyslexia are more accepted. You might sometimes still meet people who do not understand or who have incorrect ideas about dyslexia. Their comments might hurt, but that is not a reason to keep your dyslexia a secret. Instead, try to educate those people so they understand. You will be doing them a favor, as well as helping yourself and others with dyslexia.

You need to help other people help you. Let others understand how you experience the world by describing what you see, hear, and feel. Try to be as specific as possible, giving examples

FOCUS ON THE GOAL

Rob Langston described a demonstration he does during his talks to students and teachers about dyslexia. He balances two wooden boards on cinder blocks and then breaks the boards with his hand. To break the boards, he does not focus on them. Instead, he focuses on the floor below, he says. "Then I simply thrust my hand down to where I'm aiming, at the floor, and it goes effortlessly through the obstacles, the boards. When you break through obstacles, you have to focus on the positive, not the negative. If you focus on getting what you want, you will pass through the obstacles and only notice them when you are on the other side."[2]

and telling stories. Explain what you need from other people. Don't assume they should know automatically what to say and do.

You should also remember other people have their own fears, worries, and challenges. Take time to listen to them and offer your support. Consider finding volunteer work that matches your personal interests. Many successful adults with dyslexia find reaching out to others helps them feel good. By accepting and offering support, you build a strong community.

BUILDING SOCIAL SKILLS

The brain wiring that causes some people to struggle with language can also make it hard to process social cues. This means you may have trouble understanding what is being said and expressing yourself clearly. You may also be confused by nonverbal communication, such as gestures and facial expressions. If you find social interactions uncomfortable or confusing, counseling can help you improve your social skills. Trusted friends and family members can also help. Explain the situation and ask people to give you feedback. If you're not sure how someone feels, ask them.

ASK YOURSELF THIS

- *How can one child's diagnosis of dyslexia affect other family members? Have you seen this in your family?*

- *How can dyslexia affect relationships between friends? Have you ever felt stress between you and a friend because one of you had a learning disability?*

- *Can you think of anyone else who might be affected by your dyslexia?*

- *Have you tried talking to someone else with dyslexia? Did you learn something or feel better after the conversation? Who else can you go to for expert advice?*

- *What are the advantages of talking openly about your dyslexia? Have you done this? How did other people react? Would you do things differently next time?*

YOUR FUTURE

Isaac is studying journalism in college. Many people are surprised when they learn he is dyslexic and planning to be a writer. He often has to explain that being dyslexic doesn't mean he is unable to write. Assignments may take longer, but he writes and reads for fun.

Some people find that working with their dyslexia makes them stronger students.

Throughout high school, he blogged about the challenges of living with dyslexia.

After college, he wants to focus on science writing. He enjoys helping others understand difficult concepts. He can also use his writing to advocate for understanding and help for those with dyslexia. He hopes to become a role model to other young people with learning disabilities. Through his work as a journalist, he will be able to set an example of what a person with dyslexia can do.

Some of Isaac's classmates had trouble adjusting to college life. They missed classes or failed to turn in homework. Isaac had to adjust to independence, too, living on his own without his mother's constant help. Still, he had developed discipline from his years of dealing with dyslexia. He keeps careful track of his schedule to avoid missing classes or assignments. He also followed his mother's example to deal with the school system. She always helped him find teachers who would work with his learning style. Now he talks to professors in advance to figure out which ones will work best for him.

Isaac believes his dyslexia is part of the reason he will succeed. It forced him to accept his differences and ask for help when he needed it. Most important, he learned to keep trying. His focus and dedication help him show others his learning disability will not hold him back.

GETTING READY TO GO

Despite the challenges students with dyslexia face in the educational system, many have enjoyable and productive college years. If this is your path, start preparing early to make your transition smooth.

If you have an official diagnosis of dyslexia, your IEP team should be planning for your future throughout high school. This means deciding whether or not you are college bound. If you are, you should focus on developing the skills you will need there. Your team will help, but you will need to make more decisions on your own and become your own advocate. You may need to reduce the

APPLYING FOR COLLEGE

If you are going to college, should you mention your learning disability on your college application? You are not required to do so, and the college is not allowed to ask on the application form. However, in some cases it might help you to disclose your dyslexia. Maybe you feel it has had a negative effect on your grades or test scores, but you believe you can do college-level work. In that case, you might want to explain the situation to the admissions office. Before you decide, discuss the matter with your family. Your school counselor, tutor, or other experts can also have advice for you.

accommodations you receive in high school to prepare for college-level learning.

Whether or not you are heading to college, you should be developing the skills needed to survive on your own. These include time management, organization, and independence.

Once you have been accepted to a college, it is your responsibility to arrange for learning accommodations. Often the college admissions packet includes information about the offices that help students with disabilities. If you do not get this information quickly, ask for it, as you may need to request services in advance.

Knowing your rights can help you handle problems when they arise. Federal, state, and local laws protect your rights. You can find details online through the US Department of Education's Office for Civil Rights. The college's office for disabled student services can also provide you with information on laws and campus regulations.

TAKING CHARGE

You will enjoy college more if you choose a major that interests you and uses your strengths. You probably need extra time to study, so don't overwhelm yourself with a heavy class load. It is better to plan a couple of extra years to graduate than to fail classes, which will cause you to take longer anyway. If you must take especially hard classes, consider taking one class at a time during the summer. That way you can focus on a single class.

Once classes start, use the in-class and study skills you developed in high school. Try to schedule classes that suit your best time of day for learning. Prepare for each class by reading ahead. Sit in the front row if possible and try to stay focused. Study every day instead of waiting until the week before midterms or finals to cram. Join or start a study group if that works for you, and meet with tutors or the class aid as needed. Use assistive technology, such as books on tape and voice recognition software.

The most important key to college success is perseverance. Accept setbacks and learn from your mistakes while celebrating successes along the way. Like many students, you may change your mind about what you want to study. Switching to another major or even another college might be the right choice for you. That doesn't mean you have failed; it means you have taken one more step along the path to success.

OTHER TRAINING OPTIONS

Vocational programs at community and junior colleges provide an alternative to college or university. These programs are designed to

Staying organized and arranging learning accommodations are important for being successful in college.

prepare you for employment in a specific field. You could train to be a machinist, welder, mason, or carpenter. Some programs prepare students to be a medical or veterinary technician or a dental or nursing assistant. Other fields include high-tech manufacturing, electronics, and computer programming.

Technical colleges also offer programs in specific fields. These institutes focus on skills training and hands-on experience. Programs include law enforcement, car maintenance, business management, and social services.

LEARNING A TRADE

Internships and apprenticeships can help you explore career options. These experiences let you observe and assist people on the job. You can receive hands-on work experience, training, and mentoring. You will learn about the demands of the job. This is also an opportunity to try accommodations for the job in order to figure out what would work for you.

Internships are often short term, perhaps over the summer or for one semester of school. Some may provide course credit or a small salary. An apprenticeship is typically more intensive. You might get extensive training with a skilled-trade worker such as a plumber, electrician, or builder. You might be expected to work for that employer after the apprenticeship.

Most technical, community, and junior colleges offer two-year programs.

Another option is a vocational-technical center. These offer courses of study toward a certificate in a specific field. Some vocational training programs are available to high school students. Because they focus on on-the-job skills, participants can leave high school ready to take a skilled job immediately.

Some of these schools have partnerships with local industries. This may make it easier for you to find a job, since those companies are looking to hire program graduates.

You can learn many career skills at a technical or vocational school.

ON THE JOB

Whether or not you go to college, someday you will be in the workforce. Making smart choices about your career path can help you have a great future.

Look for a field that will keep your interest so you can stay motivated. Do you prefer physical labor or intellectual pursuits? Do you enjoy interacting with people or working alone? What kinds of jobs provide those opportunities?

BEST JOBS FOR PEOPLE WITH DYSLEXIA

People with dyslexia have succeeded in every career field. Your path should depend on your individual interests and strengths. However, many people with dyslexia prefer jobs that do not emphasize strong language skills. These options can include more visually oriented jobs such as art, architecture and design; science and engineering fields; and certain aspects of medicine, such as surgery.

Next, consider how your skills match up with the jobs that interest you. You can learn on the job, but you will likely be happier if you have a job that aligns with your strengths. Your personality traits are important as well, such as whether you are outgoing or shy. Your IEP team can help you answer some of these questions.

In order to get a job, you will probably have to submit a résumé or application and go through an interview. First impressions are important here, so prepare carefully. That means studying instructions and making sure you do exactly what is asked. Get help editing any letters and résumés. A job interview can cause anxiety, so prepare by considering the questions you may be asked. Learn about the company ahead of time and make sure you understand the requirements of the job.

When you get a job, it is your choice whether you tell your coworkers about your dyslexia.

When it comes time for the interview, take a deep breath and try to be yourself! Emphasize your strengths, but be honest about your work experience and skills. You do not have to tell the employer about your dyslexia.

Whether or not you tell your coworkers about your dyslexia is up to you. You may find people are more patient and understanding once they realize your situation. Liz Fife, who worked at an investment bank, says,

> *Initially I did not mention my dyslexia to co-workers for fear that they would regret hiring me or think less of me. But as time passed I realized that I was doing myself an injustice by not speaking up. How could I expect my superiors to understand that I took longer to complete a task because of my disability and not because I was procrastinating? . . . Now when I talk about my experience with friends and colleagues they can see my determination and drive and not just my disability.[1]*

You have many choices for your future—college or university, technical or vocational schools, or heading straight into the workforce.

AVOIDING DISCRIMINATION

The Americans with Disabilities Act (ADA) protects people with disabilities on the job. An employer cannot disqualify you or discriminate against you because of your disability.

On the job, the ADA requires that individuals with disabilities are provided reasonable accommodations. These may include special equipment and services or extra or different training. However, the employer is not required to provide accommodations that are very expensive or difficult to manage.

You must tell the employer about your learning disability to be eligible for legal protections. You will also have to tell your boss if you need special accommodations. If you disclose a disability, the information is confidential and should not be shared without your consent.

Whatever path you choose for your future, preparing ahead can help you succeed.

ASK YOURSELF THIS

- *If you want to go to college, how should you prepare? When should you start planning?*

- *How can college be different from high school? What adjustments will you need to make?*

- *What other educational options do you have besides college or university? What are the differences? Where do you think you would feel most comfortable?*

- *How can you decide what job will be best for you? Which fields do you find most appealing? Why?*

- *How might your dyslexia affect you on the job?*

REACHING OUT

Cameron knew a lot about learning disabilities because her brother had dyslexia. Despite the stress this sometimes caused at home, Cameron loved her brother and knew he was a wonderful person.

Sticking up for someone else can make you feel good, too.

One day in the lunchroom, the topic of learning disabilities came up. One boy said, "Dyslexics can't read. They must be really dumb." A couple of other students laughed and nodded. Cameron was tempted to let it go because she didn't want to challenge these popular kids. Yet it bothered her that someone would have such mistaken ideas.

She took a deep breath and spoke up. "My brother has dyslexia and he knows how to read." The other students looked at her in surprise, so she went on. "He works very hard at school. It takes him longer to do his homework, but his grades are all right. In some classes, he does better than I do. He's also a great musician. He made the jazz band this year."

The other students looked at the boy who'd made the rude comment. His face was red. "Sorry," he mumbled. "I didn't mean to insult your brother. I don't really know much about dyslexia."

Another girl said, "I have dyslexia, too." This girl was in the advanced classes and few people had guessed she had a learning disability. "I don't usually talk about it." She smiled at Cameron. "But I'm glad you said something. I was too embarrassed."

HOW DO I KNOW IF SOMEBODY IS DYSLEXIC?

If someone shows several of the characteristics described in chapters 1 and 2, they may have dyslexia. However, only trained professionals can give a definite diagnosis. The common signs of dyslexia are only possible indicators, not proof.

The students began an honest discussion of dyslexia. Because Cameron spoke up, she helped others understand what dyslexia is really like. She also began a closer friendship with her classmate with dyslexia, who had often seemed shy.

EQUALLY UNIQUE

Have you ever met someone who seemed odd or different? Maybe he wouldn't look you in the eye, or she stood too close and made too much eye contact. Maybe he seemed confused or distracted, unable to follow your conversation. Maybe she changed the subject suddenly, as if she wasn't interested in your thoughts.

You might have wondered if the person was ignoring you or making fun of you. Maybe you felt uncomfortable or even angry and didn't want to talk to them anymore. But before you judge someone, try to understand what is really going on. If the person is dyslexic, he or she may struggle with social interactions. The brain wiring that makes it hard to process written language also makes it difficult to process verbal and nonverbal cues. People with dyslexia may also have less experience with social interactions because they need to spend more time on schoolwork.

That doesn't mean all people with dyslexia are socially awkward! Some are charming, outgoing, and likable. Yet they may still think and react differently in subtle ways that are sometimes puzzling.

If you want to have a better understanding of the challenges faced by students with learning disabilities, try this exercise. Hold a piece of paper on your forehead and then write your name on it with your nondominant hand. Beth Fissel, who has children with dyslexia, suggested this experiment. In another simulation, she mixes up the directions for the game Simon Says so they don't make sense. These examples help people without learning

HOW WORDS LOOK TO PEOPLE WITH DYSLEXIA

Writing can look different to someone who has dyslexia:

Ma yb ethew ordsar e notsp elle dcor rectly.

Maybethewordsareallpushedtogether.

Ma b tha wrdz r spelt jist az tha sond.

People with dyslexia may also think in pictures rather than in words. This means they can get a word wrong, such as reading cat when it actually says *kitten*. Or they may understand the meaning but be unable to remember the word. In addition, words that do not have clear mental pictures, such as *if* or *when*, can cause confusion.

Whether you have dyslexia or someone you know does, being kind and compassionate will help improve your relationships.

disabilities understand the frustrations of dyslexia.

If someone you know is open about his or her dyslexia, feel free to ask questions about his or her experiences. This can help you better understand how that person sees the world. It can also help the person with dyslexia feel more comfortable and accepted.

Communication is important, for both you and your friends or relatives with dyslexia. Try to patiently and clearly express what you want and need. Remember that someone with dyslexia might have trouble following or remembering what you say. Ask for feedback to make sure the other person understands. If you have a good relationship, you might gently offer suggestions about social behavior. People can be sensitive about their learning disabilities, but chances are they also want to know how to maintain relationships.

SPEAK UP

You can also help people with learning disabilities by speaking up when someone is teased. School bullying is a common problem affecting at least 20 percent of students in the United States.[1] Many people believe that children with special needs, including the learning disabled, are bullied more than others.

Bullying can involve physical confrontations, verbal insults, online harassment, or refusing to let the victim participate in activities. "Bystanders often feel uncomfortable intervening; they're glad they're not the target and don't want to be picked on next," explains Eve Kessler, an advocate for children with special educational needs. "But without bystander support, the targets feel abandoned while bullies feel supported."[2]

We all have a responsibility to stop bullying. If you are afraid to stand up to the bully directly, report the situation to your parents or school

BULLYING AND LEARNING DISABILITIES

Every state has official laws or policies on bullying. The details vary between states, but most offer guidelines on identifying bullying, setting consequences, and providing help for victims. The federal government also offers protection under Section 504 of the Rehabilitation Act and Title II of the Americans with Disabilities Act of 1990. If you are a victim of bullying, start by alerting your school. The school should eliminate the hostile environment and discipline the harassers. If you do not get adequate help, the school can be held accountable.

officials. The entire community must work together to put an end to bullying.

We all have our unique quirks, which is what makes people so interesting. You can help others feel comfortable by reaching out and accepting their differences.

Sometimes you may feel overwhelmed by your own problems. You may think you don't have time for anything beyond your own schoolwork, job, chores, and relationships. But it is important to help others, for their sakes and for your own.

As dyslexia advocate Rob Langston says, "When you succeed, you have to share your success with others and help those who come after you."[3] Reach out to other students who have dyslexia. Share the lessons you have learned and support each other. By helping others, you will also help yourself. You will develop friendships and build communication skills. You will feel better about yourself because you are having a positive effect on the world.

ASK YOURSELF THIS

- *How can you identify a dyslexic person? Should you talk to them about it? Why or why not?*

- *Why might dyslexic and non-dyslexic people have trouble communicating? What can they do to understand each other?*

- *What are the advantages to talking openly with others about your misunderstandings? Is this easy or hard to do? How can you feel more comfortable being open?*

- *Have you ever witnessed bullying? Do you think you have ever bullied someone else or been bullied yourself? Why might someone act like a bully? What can you do if you witness bullying?*

- *What are the advantages to helping other people? Do you ever do volunteer work? How does that make you feel?*

JUST THE FACTS

Dyslexia is a learning disability caused by differences in the brain. It can have many effects, but it typically impairs a person's ability to read.

Dyslexia causes problems in processing information. That can affect language, including reading, writing, and spelling. Dyslexia may also cause difficulties in math, reasoning, organizational abilities, and attention. Some people with dyslexia struggle with nonverbal communication as well.

Dyslexia is a genetic condition, a difference in the way the brain develops and functions. People with dyslexia appear to have less gray matter in part of the brain. Many people with dyslexia also have structural differences in white matter compared to average readers. People with dyslexia may also have different brain symmetry.

Dyslexia tends to run in families. For people with attention deficit/hyperactivity disorder (ADHD), there's a 60 percent chance of also having dyslexia.

According to some estimates, 10 to 15 percent of the US population has dyslexia. The percentage of people who have a language-based learning disability may be as high as 20 percent.

People with dyslexia often show strengths. Students with dyslexia often do well in science, math, computer programming, and technology. Some may be good at arts and crafts.

A thorough differential diagnosis involves a series of tests. These study how the subject expresses and understands oral and written language. They test sight and hearing, intellectual functioning, cognitive processing, and educational achievement. They adjust for family history and social environment.

After testing, specific recommendations are made based on individual needs. A team meeting with the subject's family, testers, and teachers results in a plan of action. An Individualized Education Program (IEP) lists the special education services the child will receive from the school.

Because dyslexia is a biological condition rather than a disease, there is no cure. Proper treatment provides the education that best suits the dyslexic brain and learning style. Treatment may focus on instruction in phonemic awareness and phonics. This training must be intense and long lasting.

Classroom or work accommodations can help people with dyslexia succeed. Written instructions, or a tape recorder or other devices to record lessons and directions, allow for later review. A reading guide can help students focus on relevant material. Assignment books, calendars, and graphic organizers aid with organization.

The Individuals with Disabilities Education Act (IDEA) identifies a number of disabilities. If a child needs special education and related services because of a disability, IDEA ensures the child receives help. Section 504 of the Rehabilitation Act and the Americans with Disabilities Act (ADA) provide additional protections.

WHERE TO TURN

If You Need Information and Support

Dyslexia is a complex condition, but many organizations provide information and assistance. Dyslexia Help at the University of Michigan offers information for individuals with dyslexia as well as parents and professionals: http://dyslexiahelp.umich.edu/

The dyslexia page at TeensHealth offers studying, note taking, and test taking tips for teens with an audio option: http://kidshealth.org/teen/school_jobs/school/dyslexia.html

The International Dyslexia Association (IDA) allows you to search for tutors, dyslexia specialists, and other professionals in your state: http://www.interdys.org/

Several organizations offer ongoing help to adults with learning disabilities. These include the Learning Disabilities Association of America (http://www.ldanatl.org/) and the Association on Higher Education and Disability (AHEAD) (http://www.ahead.org/).

If You Need Accessible Instructional Materials

Modern technology offers many tools that can help those with learning disabilities read and write. Bookshare offers audio books, including textbooks and newspapers. Membership is free for students, with more than 140,000 titles available: https://www.bookshare.org/. Learning Ally offers more than 75,000 digitally recorded audiobooks, including textbooks: http://www.learningally.org/. Headstrong Nation provides technology tools designed for dyslexics: http://www.headstrongnation.org/tools

If You Need Legal Help

If you require special accommodations at school or work, the law protects you. The Individuals with Disabilities Education Act (IDEA) provides help for children who need special education services. Visit the US Department of Education at http://idea.ed.gov/. Section 504 of the Rehabilitation

Act and the Americans with Disabilities Act (ADA) provide additional protections. Visit the US Department of Justice at http://www.ada.gov/cguide.htm. You can learn more about these laws and others at the National Center for Learning Disabilities Web site at http://www.ncld.org.

If You Are Feeling Depressed

If you have frequent negative thoughts about yourself and feel hopeless about the future, you may have depression. Talk to your parents, counselor, or doctor if you feel depressed. A professional counselor can help you understand and manage your feelings. Support groups can offer advice and help you meet people who understand your situation. The International Dyslexia Association lists some groups and events: http://www.interdys.org/

Identifying and nurturing your strengths can also help with depression. Try taking classes such as art, music, and drama, or joining clubs. Celebrate successes and reach out to others through volunteer work.

If You Are a Victim of Bullying

Alert your school if you are bullied or witness bullying. The school should discipline the bullies and provide a safer environment. If you do not get adequate help, the school can be held accountable. Every state has official laws or policies on bullying. The government also offers protection under Section 504 of the Rehabilitation Act and Title II of the Americans with Disabilities Act of 1990.

The education program WINGS for kids offers an antibullying kit targeted at parents and teachers: http://www.wingsforkids.org/files/Full%20Bully%20Kit.pdf

GLOSSARY

accommodation
Something that can be done to help a disabled student learn and be fairly evaluated.

advocate
A person who pleads for help on someone else's behalf.

attention-deficit/hyperactivity disorder (ADHD)
A condition characterized by behavioral difficulties that may interfere with school, work, and social life.

cognitive
Related to knowing, perceiving, remembering, judging, and reasoning.

compensate
To counterbalance, offset, or provide an equivalent.

differential diagnosis
A method of diagnosing a disease or disorder by considering all possible causes of symptoms.

functionally illiterate
Having reading and writing skills not sufficient for daily needs.

intervention
In medical terms, a measure intended to improve health.

orally
Spoken rather than written.

phonemic awareness
The ability to manipulate sounds, such as blending sounds to form new words or segmenting words into sounds.

phonics
How sounds relate to letters.

transpose
To transfer one into the place of another, as in putting letters in the wrong order.

ADDITIONAL RESOURCES

SELECTED BIBLIOGRAPHY

"The Dyslexia Toolkit." *National Center for Learning Disabilities*. National Center for Learning Disabilities, 2013. PDF.

Langston, Rob. *For the Children: Redefining Success in School and Success in Life*. Austin, TX: TurnKey, 2002. Print.

FURTHER READINGS

Grossberg, Blythe. *Applying to College for Students with ADD or LD: A Guide to Keep You (And Your Parents) Sane, Satisfied, and Organized Through the Admissions Process*. Washington, DC: Magination, 2010. Print.

Mannix, Darlene. *Life Skills Activities for Secondary Students with Special Needs*. 2nd ed. San Francisco, CA: Jossey-Bass, 2009. Print.

Paquette, Penny Hutchins, and Cheryl Gerson Tuttle. *Learning Disabilities: The Ultimate Teen Guide*. Lanham, MD: Scarecrow, 2006. Print.

WEB SITES

To learn more about living with dyslexia, visit ABDO
Publishing Company online at **www.abdopublishing.com**.
Web sites about living with dyslexia are featured on our Book
Links page. These links are routinely monitored and updated
to provide the most current information available.

SOURCE NOTES

CHAPTER 1. WHAT IS DYSLEXIA?

1. "Q: How Common Are Language-Based Disabilities?" *The International Dyslexia Association*. International Dyslexia Association, n.d. Web. 25 July 2013.

2. "The Dyslexia Research Institute Mission." *Dyslexia Research Institute*. Dyslexia Research Institute, n.d. Web. 25 July 2013.

3. "Identification: Dyslexia." *Dyslexia Research Institute*. Dyslexia Research Institute, n.d. Web. 25 July 2013.

CHAPTER 2. EXTRA CHALLENGES

None.

CHAPTER 3. THE BRIGHT SIDE OF DYSLEXIA

1. Meghan Neal. "Dyslexia's Special Club: Orlando Bloom Speaks Out." *Huffington Post*. Huffington Post, 17 Nov 2011. Web. 25 July 2013.

2. Chris Warren. "Coudl This Be teh Sercet to Sussecc?" *American Airline's American Way* July 2008. Web. *Yale Center for Dyslexia and Creativity*. 25 July 2013.

3. Rob Langston. *For the Children, Redefining Success in School and Success in Life*. Austin, TX: TurnKey, 2002. Print. 3.

4. "The Dyslexia Toolkit." *National Center for Learning Disabilities*. National Center for Learning Disabilities, n.d. PDF. 36. 16 Apr 2013.

5. Susan Baum. "Focusing on Strengths Benefits Children with LD and ADHD." *Smart Kids with Learning Disabilities*. Smart Kids with Learning Disabilities, 6 Feb 2012. Web. 25 July 2013.

CHAPTER 4. TESTING AND DIAGNOSIS

1. Rob Langston. *For the Children, Redefining Success in School and Success in Life*. Austin, TX: TurnKey, 2002. Print. 104.

CHAPTER 5. WHAT'S HAPPENING IN MY BRAIN?

1. "Myth #17: The Defining Feature of Dyslexia Is Reversing Letters." *Association for Psychological Science.* Association for Psychological Science, n.d. Web. 25 July 2013.

2. Sally Shaywitz, MD. "Dyslexia." *Scientific American* Nov. 1996. *Yale Center for Dyslexia and Creativity*. 25 July 2013.

SOURCE NOTES CONTINUED

CHAPTER 6. DYSLEXIA AT SCHOOL

None.

CHAPTER 7. HELP AT HOME

None.

CHAPTER 8. COPING AND SUPPORT

1. "The Dyslexia Toolkit." *National Center for Learning Disabilities.* National Center for Learning Disabilities, n.d. PDF. 35. 16 Apr 2013.

2. Rob Langston. *For the Children, Redefining Success in School and Success in Life.* Austin, TX: TurnKey, 2002. Print. 9.

CHAPTER 9. YOUR FUTURE

1. Liz Fife. Personal Story: Disclosing LD in the Workplace. 26 Apr 2013. http://www.ncld.org/learning-disability-resources/special-needs-stories/adults-with-ld/disclosing-ld-workplace

CHAPTER 10. REACHING OUT

1. Eve Kessler. Bullying: Kids with LD Are Easy Targets. Smart Kids with Learning Disabilities. Web. 29 Apr 2013. http://www.smartkidswithld.org/ld-basics/beyond-the-classroom/bullying-kids-with-ld-are-easy-targets

2. Eve Kessler. Bullying: Kids with LD Are Easy Targets. Smart Kids with Learning Disabilities. Web. 29 Apr 2013. http://www.smartkidswithld.org/ld-basics/beyond-the-classroom/bullying-kids-with-ld-are-easy-targets

3. Rob Langston. *For the Children, Redefining Success in School and Success in Life*. Austin, TX: TurnKey, 2002. Print. 61.

INDEX

ABOUT THE AUTHOR

Chris Eboch writes fiction and nonfiction for all ages. Her recent nonfiction titles include *The Green Movement* and *Magnets in the Real World*. Her novels for young people include historical fiction, ghost stories, and action-packed adventures. Learn more about her work at www.chriseboch.com.